Olympiad Planner 2

for

(MATHEMATICS, SCIENCE, CYBER, AND ENGLISH OLYMPIADS)

Editorial Board

V&S PUBLISHERS

Published by:

V&S PUBLISHERS

F-2/16, Ansari road, Daryaganj, New Delhi-110002
☎ 23240026, 23240027 • *Fax:* 011-23240028
Email: info@vspublishers.com • *Website:* www.vspublishers.com

Regional Office : Hyderabad
5-1-707/1, Brij Bhawan (Beside Central Bank of India Lane)
Bank Street, Koti, Hyderabad - 500 095
☎ 040-24737290
E-mail: vspublishershyd@gmail.com

Branch Office : Mumbai
Jaywant Industrial Estate, 2nd Floor–222, Tardeo Road
Opposite Sobo Central Mall, Mumbai – 400 034
☎ 022-23510736
E-mail: vspublishersmum@gmail.com

Follow us on:

All books available at **www.vspublishers.com**

ISBN 978-93-579408-9-4

Printed at : Param Offseters Okhla New Delhi-110020

Publisher's Note

V&S Publishers, after the grand success of a number of Academic and General books, is pleased to bring out Olympiad Planners for classes from 1st to 10th under The Gen X series – generating Xcellence in generation X – which helps students to prepare for the Olympiad exams. The planner provides step-wise guidance to go through the exam i.e. *how to register, tips and study chart for efficient preparation, pattern and syllabus of exam, recommended study material and scholarships.* One model paper on Mathematics, Science, Cyber and English Olympiad each has been included for practice purpose.

All planners have been developed to provide systematic guidance to the students who aspire to become Olympiad champs at national and international levels. To get success in Olympiads, students need to do thorough study of topics covered in Olympiad syllabus and the topics covered in school syllabus as well. The tips and tricks given in this planner help candidates to prepare for the exam efficiently. Olympiads check efficiency of candidates in problem solving. These exams are conducted in different stages at regional, national, and international levels. At each stage of the exam, a candidate should be fully prepared to take new challenges. Thus, this exam requires careful attention towards comprehension of concepts and thorough practice.

We wish you all success in the examination and a very bright future.

All the best

Contents

1 Intorduction to Olympiad

International Mathematical Olympiad (IMO)

International Mathematical Olympiad (IMO) is a world championship mathematics competition for students of High School and it is held annually in different countries. The first IMO with seven participating countries was held in 1959 in Romania. The scope of this exam was gradually expanded to over 100 countries within five continents. The IMO Advisory Board ensures that the competition takes place every year and that each host country observes regulations and traditions of the IMO.

In India, Mathematics Olympiad is conducted by **Homi Bhabha Centre for Science Education (HBCSE)** which organises this exam on behalf of **National Board for Higher Mathematics (NBHM)** of the Department of Atomic Energy (DAE). **Central Board of Secondary Education (CBSE)** also conducts Group Mathematical Olympiad based on which successful candidates are sent to the International Mathematical Olympiad. A maximum of 30 students from CBSE group are selected (strictly in order of merit) to participate in Indian National Mathematical Olympiad (INMO) conducted by National Board of Higher Mathematics (NBHM). The selection at national level leads to participation at International Mathematical Olympiad. **Science Olympiad Foundation (SOF)** which identifies and encourages mathematical creativity of children also conducts Mathematics Olympiad in schools across India and abroad.

The students from classes 1–12 are eligible to appear in Maths Olympiad. For classes 1–4, 10 questions from Section–1 (Logical Reasoning), 10 questions from Section–2 (Mathematical Reasoning), 10 questions from Section–3 (Everyday Mathematics) and 5 questions from Section–4 (Achievers section) are asked. Thus, the students are required to answer 35 questions in 60 minutes.

For classes 5–12, 15 questions from Section–1 (Logical Reasoning), 20 questions from Section–2 (Mathematical Reasoning), 10 questions from Section–3 (Everyday Mathematics) and 5 questions from Section–4 (Achievers section) are asked. Thus, the students are required to answer 50 questions in 60 minutes.

National Science Olympiad (NSO)

The National Science Olympiad (NSO) is a science competition in Asia. It is conducted in two levels. The students from classes 1–12 are eligible to appear in it. For classes 1– 4, 5 questions from Section–1 (Logical Reasoning) and 25 questions from Section–2 (Science) and 5 questions from Section–3 (Achievers section) are asked in the exam. Thus, the students are required to answer 35 questions in 60 minutes. For classes 5–10, 10 questions from Section–1 (Logical Reasoning) and 35 questions from Section–2 (Science) and 5 questions from Section–3 (Achievers section) are asked. Thus, the students are required to answer 50 questions in 60 minutes. The questions are of Multiple Choice Questions (MCQs) type and students are required to mark their responses on OMR answer sheets.

All the students participating in NSO (1st level) get a Student Performance Report (SPR), with their Score, School Rank, City Rank, State Rank, International Rank and Percentile, as well as a Certificate of Participation. SOF also generates a performance report for all participating schools, known as School Performance Report (SCPR). On the basis of 1st level exam, Gold, Silver and Bronze medals are awarded to 1st, 2nd and 3rd rank holder (with minimum 10 enrolments in the concerned class) and Gold medal to every class topper (if 5–9 students have enrolled) in each participating school. Selected students appear for 2nd level examination and according to 2nd level ranks, the prizes are given. The criteria for selection to 2nd level are as follows: the student should have secured International Rank from 1–500 (both inclusive) and/or State Rank from 1–10 (both inclusive) and/or Student should secure 1st, 2nd or 3rd rank (minimum ten enrollments) and/or a minimum of 30% of total marks. All students participating in NSO (2nd level) are also given a Certificate of Merit. The respective school of each student with International Rank from 1–3 (both inclusive) is awarded a Science Intellect Trophy (SIT) for having the winning students on their rolls.

Thus, Olympiad is a platform that identifies young geniuses and provides them with a unique competitive platform where they can prove themselves.

National Cyber Olympiad (NCO)

National Cyber Olympiad (NCO) is an international championship competition that identifies Cyber Savvy talents. The NCO is an academic and scholastic aptitude competition which is held to identify extraordinary skills of students and to provide them a distinction. This exam is conducted to search talented students in computer education and to encourage them to develop their careers in this field. The students from classes 2–12 are eligible to appear in it. It is conducted in two levels. At the 1st level of exam, for classes 2–4, 5 questions from Section–1 (Logical Reasoning), 25 questions from Section–2 (Computer and IT) and 25 questions from Section–3 (Achievers section) are asked whereas for classes 5–12, 10 questions from Section–1 (Logical Reasoning), 35 questions from Section–2 (Computer and IT), 5 questions from Section–3 (Achievers section) are asked. The students are required to answer a total of 50 questions in 60 minutes and there is no negative marking for incorrect answers. Questions are of Multiple Choice Questions (MCQs) type and students are required to mark their responses on OMR answer sheets.

In India, NCO is conducted by Science Olympiad Foundation (SOF) which identifies and encourages children to enhance their skills in Cyber and IT. This exam assesses a student at national level. The national level assessment gives students a fair idea of the position where he/she stands in comparison to other students and inspires him/her to score better marks.

International English Olympiad (IEO)

International English Olympiad (IEO) is an examination of the first of its kind in the history of English language testing in India. The IEO is a joint venture of the Science Olympiad Foundation and The English and Foreign Languages University (EFLU), Hyderabad. The examination has been developed by a group of professionals who constitute the All India English Language Testing Authority (AIELTA) at The English and Foreign Languages University (EFLU).

The students from classes 1–12 are eligible to appear in International English Olympiad. For classes 1–4, 30 MCQs from Sections 1–3 (Word and Structure Knowledge, Reading, Spoken and Written Expression) and 5 MCQs from Section–4 (Achievers section) are asked whereas for classes 5–12, 45 MCQs are asked from Sections 1–3 (Word and Structure Knowledge, Reading and Spoken and Written Expression) and 5 MCQs from Section–4 (Achievers section) are asked.

2 How to Apply

Registration: The IMO is open to students from 1st to 12th standard. The prospectus containing the registration forms is sent to all the schools which are registered with SOF. The schools which are not registered may also request for prospectus by sending an e-mail at *info@sofworld.org* or by making a phone call to SOF.

Registration of New Schools: The schools which want to participate in the Olympiad are required to send their complete address in the following format.

- School Name : ____________
- Address : ____________
- City : ____________
- State : ____________
- Pin code : ____________
- Phone No. with STD Code : ____________
- E-mail : ____________
- Principal's Name : ____________

The SOF will send relevant information and registration forms to the school at appropriate time. The registration forms duly filled in and complete in all respects must be submitted to the SOF by the due date. Last date of receipt of registrations is 30 days before the chosen date of exam.

Roll Numbers: The school's coordinator (teacher) generates students' Roll Numbers as per the guidelines. A copy of these roll numbers along with the Students' Registration Sheet (SRS) and School Registration Form (SRF) should be sent to the Foundation's office on/before the due date of submission of forms. The Foundation will register the applicant school and the students and will dispatch question papers and guidelines for conducting the examination.

Note: Principals/teachers of all participating schools may please note that any school can be registered as a centre for IMO. No fee is required from the institution to be a registered examination centre. For a school to become the centre, at least 10 students need to be registered from the school for feasibility reasons. The IMO is conducted in two days for Level 1. Every school may select a date for conducting the IMO exam as per its convenience. A different question paper will be provided to the students on each day.

The students should register through their respective schools only. An individual registration by students is not acceptable.

Fee Structure

For schools in India: A nominal fee is charged from each student. The school shall retain a part of it per student per Olympiad for its expenses as exam centre. The details about fee/mode of payment etc. are given in detail in Registration Forms sent to the schools.

Mode of Payment: The school can make payment via Demand Draft or through NEFT/ RTGS

- **Demand Draft:** It should be made in favour of **Science Olympiad Foundation** payable at **New Delhi.**
- **NEFT/ RTGS:** Details for NEFT/RTGS are:
    - Beneficiary Name : Science Olympiad Foundation
    - Beneficiary A/C No. : SOFXXXXXX (XXXXXX denotes school Code allotted by Science Olympiad Foundation)
    - Beneficiary Bank Name : ICICI Bank
    - Beneficiary Branch : CMS
    - IFSC Code : ICIC0000103

Schedule of Examination

The schools may select a date for conducting the Olympiads in their school premises. The change in date is not permitted. There are separate question papers for different dates. The participating schools may send registrations latest by 31st August every year.

For knowing the date and schedule of exam, students are advised to contact the co-ordinator of their school.

OR

Visit www.sofworld.org for updates on dates, schedule, and pattern of exam etc.

The schedule of Olympiad exams for 2015-16 is as follows:

1st Level Exams:

EXAM NAME	DATE 1	DATE 2
15th NCO	23rd Sept 2015	8th Oct 2015
18th NSO	20th Oct 2015	5th Nov 2015
9th IMO	26th Nov 2015	10th Dec 2015
6th IEO	20th Jan 2016	28th Jan 2016

2nd Level Exams:

2nd level exam was held on 2nd/ 3rd Sunday of Feb 2016. The 2nd level exam is held for students from classes 3rd to 12th for NCO, NSO and IMO. IEO is a single level exam.

3 Selection Procedure

Selection Procedure for IMO

The selection of student would be done on the basis of performance in the exam. Results of both levels of IMO are declared within 6 weeks of the examination.

- The results are sent to the concerned schools.
- The results are also made available on SOF's website.

International Mathematics Olympiad is conducted in 2 Levels/phases.

Level 1: The first level of the test is organized in the respective schools of the participants during school hours.

(i) The level 1 competition is a written objective type test of 60 minutes' duration comprising 35 objective-type (Multiple Choice) questions for class 2 to class 4 and 50 objective-type (Multiple Choice) questions for class 5 to class 12.

(ii) The question paper consists of:

(a) Logical Reasoning (b) Mathematical Reasoning (c) Everyday Mathematics (d) Achievers Section

(iii) There are separate question papers for each class.

(iv) The medium of the test is English.

(v) CBSE, ICSE/ISC and State Board syllabus is followed for setting the test papers.

(vi) The exam is conducted during school hours.

Level 2: The qualifiers to second round include the following:

(i) Top 5% of candidates class-wise, who appear for the 1st level exam. Due weight-age to marks scored in different sections will be given. Each section is accorded with separate weight-age.

(ii) State-wise top 10 rank holders class-wise.

(iii) Class topper where at least 10 students from a class appear in the exam and scores 75% qualifying marks.

Selection Procedure for NSO

Level 1: The first level of the test is organized in respective schools of participants during school hours.

(i) The level 1 competition is a written objective type test of 60 minutes duration comprising 35 objective type (Multiple Choice) questions for class 2 to class 4 and 50 objective type (Multiple Choice) questions for class 5 to class 12.

(ii) The question paper for class 1st to class 10th consists of:

(a) Logical Reasoning (b) Science (c) Achievers section

(iii) There are separate question papers for each class.

(iv) The medium of the test is English.

(v) CBSE, ICSE/ISC and State Board syllabus is followed for setting test papers.

(vi) The exam is conducted during school hours.

Level 2: The qualifiers to second round would include the following:

(i) Top 5% of candidates class-wise, who appear for the 1st level exam. Due weight-age to marks scored in different sections will be given. Each section is accorded with separate weight-age.

(ii) State-wise top 10 rank holders class-wise.

(iii) Class topper where at least 10 students from a class appear in the exam scores 75% qualifying marks.

Selection Procedure for NCO

National Cyber Olympiad is conducted in 2 Levels

Level 1: The first level of the test is organized in respective schools of participants during school hours.

(i) The level 1 competition is a written objective type test of 60 minutes duration comprising 35 objective type (Multiple Choice) questions for class 2 to class 4 and 50 objective type (Multiple Choice) questions for class 5 to class 12.

(ii) The question paper consists of :

(a) Logical Reasoning
(b) Computer and Information Technology
(c) Achievers Section

(iii) There are separate question papers for each class.

(iv) The medium of the test is English.

(v) CBSE, ICSE/ISC and State Board syllabus is followed for setting the test papers.

(vi) The exam is conducted during school hours.

Level 2: The qualifiers to second round would include the following

(i) Top 5% students who appear for the 1st level exam from every class

(ii) State-wise top 10 performing students from each class

(iii) Topper of each class where at least 10 students have appeared for the exam

Selection Procedure for IEO

Criteria for ranking in 2nd level Olympiad exams:

In case of 2nd level exams, ranks will be accorded on the basis of following criteria:

(i) Total Marks scored in 2nd level exam

In case of a tie of marks, ranks will be finalized as per following order:

(a) Marks scored in sections of 2nd level exam accord more priority.

(b) Total Marks scored in level 1 exam

(c) Marks scored in sections in level 1 exam accord more priority

(d) Past performance of student

(e) Date of Birth - Younger student gets higher priority

Note: In 2nd level, no two students will be given the same rank.

Criteria for ranking- single level Olympiad exams:

For IEO and class 1 and 2 students appearing in NCO, NSO and/or IMO exams, ranks will be accorded on the following criteria:

(i) Marks obtained in the exam.

In case two or more students score same number of marks, ranks will be determined on the following criteria:

(a) Marks obtained in different sections of the exam. Each section is accorded separate priority.

(b) Student's performance in school during previous year - as mentioned in the OMR. This may be verified at the discretion of SOF. Student not stating past year's performance may not be considered for ranking in case of a tie.

(c) Age of student - with greater preference being given to younger student.

(d) Telephonic or personal Interview may be conducted.

No two students will be given same rank. However, in case two or more students score equally on all parameters defined above, the award may be distributed equally among all winners.

4 Syllabus and Curriculum

IMO Class-2

Section 1: Mathematical Reasoning: Numerals and Number Name, Number Sense (3 digit numbers), Money, Measurement of Length (conversions), Weight, Time and Temperature, Calendar, Point, Line and Plane Figures.

Section 2: Logical Reasoning: Problems Based on Figures, Patterns, Series Completion, Find Odd Numeral Out, Geometrical Shapes

Section 3: Achievers Section: Higher Order Thinking Questions - from the above given Syllabus.

NSO Class-2

Section 1: Logical Reasoning: Patterns, Measuring Units, Odd One Out, Series Completion, Geometrical Shapes, Analogy, Ranking Test, Grouping of Figures, Coding-Decoding, Embedded Figures.

Section 2: Science: Plants, Animals, Human Body, Food, Housing and Clothing, Family and Festivals, Occupations, Good Habits and Safety Rules, Transport and Communication, Air, Water and Rocks, Earth and Universe.

Section 3: Achievers Section: Higher Order Thinking Questions - Syllabus as per Section–2.

NCO Class-2

Section 1: Logical Reasoning: Patterns, Measuring Units, Odd One Out, Series Completion, Geometrical Shapes, Analogy, Ranking Test, Grouping of Figures, Coding-Decoding, Embedded Figures.

Section 2: Computer and IT: Introduction to Computers, General Information about Computers, Parts of Computer, Uses of Computer, Learning to use Keyboard and Mouse, Introduction to MS-Paint, Latest Developments in the field of IT.

Section 3: Achievers Section: Higher Order Thinking Questions - Syllabus as per Section–2.

Questions are based on Windows 7 and MS-Office 2010.

IEO Class-2

Section 1: Word and Structure Knowledge: Collocations, Spellings, Words related to animals and their sounds, Clothes, Body parts, Basic emotions, Food etc. Nouns, Pronouns, Verbs, Adverbs, Adjectives, Articles, Prepositions, Conjunctions, Contractions, Word order, Punctuation, Simple tenses.

Section 2: Reading Comprehension: Search for and retrieve information from various text types like stories, short dialogues, etc. Acquire broad understanding of and look for specific information in short texts like messages, invitations, etc.

Section 3: Spoken and Written Expressions: Ability to understand situation-based variations in functions like thanking, greeting, asking for permission, introducing (oneself), etc.

Section 4 : Achievers Section: Higher Order Thinking Questions - Syllabus as per Sections 1, 2 and 3.

5 Pattern of Exam

International Mathematics Olympiad

SOF LEVEL–1

Class	Section	No. of Questions	Marks Per Question	Total Marks
1 to 4	Logical Reasoning	10	1	10
	Mathematical Reasoning	10	1	10
	Everyday Mathematics	10	1	10
	Achievers Section	5	2	10
	Grand Total	**35**		**40**
5 to 12	Logical Reasoning	15	1	15
	Mathematical Reasoning	20	1	20
	Everyday Mathematics	10	1	10
	Achievers Section	5	3	15
	Grand Total	**50**		**60**

SOF LEVEL–2

Class	Section	No. of Questions	Marks Per Question	Total Marks
3 to 4	Mathematics	30	1	30
	Achievers	5	2	10
	Grand Total	**35**		**40**
5 to 12	Mathematics	45	1	45
	Achievers Section	5	3	15
	Grand Total	**50**		**60**

National Science Olympiad

Class	Section	No. of Questions	Marks/ Question	Total Marks
1 to 4	Logical Reasoning	5	1	5
	Science	25	1	25
	Achievers Section	5	2	10
	Grand Total	**35**		**40**
5 to 10	Logical Reasoning	10	1	10
	Science	35	1	35
	Achievers Section	5	3	15
	Grand Total	**50**		**60**
11 and 12	Physics & Chemistry	25	1	25
	Achievers Section	5	3	15
	Mathematics/Biology	20	1	20
	Grand Total	**50**		**60**

National Cyber Olympiad

NCO LEVEL–1

Class	Section	No. of Questions	Marks per Question	Total Marks
2 to 4	Logical Reasoning	5	1	5
	Computers & IT	25	1	25
	Achievers Section	5	2	10
	Grand Total	**35**		**40**
5 to 12	Logical Reasoning	10	1	10
	Computers & IT	35	1	35
	Achievers Section	5	3	15
	Grand Total	**50**		**60**

NCO LEVE–2

Class	Section	No. of Questions	Marks per Question	Total Marks
3 to 4	Computers & IT	30	1	30
	Achievers Section	5	2	10
	Grand Total	**35**		**40**
5 to 12	Computers & IT	45	1	45
	Achievers Section	5	3	15
	Grand Total	**50**		**60**

International English Olympiad

Class	Section	No. of Questions	Marks per Question	Total Marks
1 to 4	Word and Structure Knowledge			
	Reading	30	1	30
	Spoken and Written Expression			
	Achievers Section	5	2	10
	Grand Total	**35**		**40**
5 to 12	Word and Structure Knowledge			
	Reading	45	1	45
	Spoken and Written Expression			
	Achievers Section	5	3	15
	Grand Total	**50**		**60**

6 Study Chart for Efficient Preparation

IMO CLASS–2

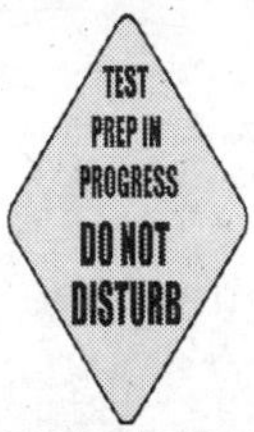	**Week 1** 	**Week 2** 	**Week 3** 	**Week 4** 
Day/Time	**Two Hours**	**Two Hours**	**Two Hours**	**Three Hours**
Monday	Numbers Sense	Money	High Order Thinking Skills	IMO 2012 SET A
Tuesday	Addition and Subtraction	Geometrical Shapes	Practice Multiple Choice Questions from Section 1	IMO 2012 SET B
Wednesday	Multiplication	Pattern	Practice Multiple Choice Questions from Section 2	IMO 2013 SET A
Thursday	Division	Series Completion	*Identify your weak areas and strengthen the same	IMO 2013 SET B
Friday	Measurement	Classification	Revision Section 1 and 2	*Identify your weak areas and strengthen the same

Saturday	Time, Calendar, and Temperature	Problems Based on Figures	Revision Section 3	Model Test Paper–1
Sunday	Revision	Revision	*Identify your weak areas and strengthen the same	Model Test Paper–2

Note:

- Identify your weak areas through detailed reports and strengthen the areas.
- Practice questions from huge question bank:
  - (i) MTG Workbooks for Class 2
  - (ii) 'SOF Olympiad Trainer' Mobile Apps
  - (iii) OSDS (Olympiad Skill Development System)
  - (iv) Olympiads' Books of Reasoning (for preparation of the reasoning of Olympiads)
  - (v) E-Quiz
- Take more mock tests to improve your efficiency and become fully prepared for the exam.

NSO CLASS–2

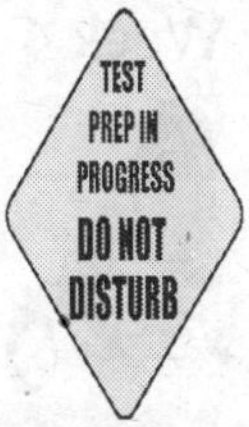	Week 1 	Week 2 	Week 3 	Week 4 
Day/Time	**Two Hours**	**Two Hours**	**Two Hours**	**Two Hours**
Monday	• Plants	• Food	• Transport and Communication	Subjective Section
Tuesday	• Analogy • Series Completion	• Coding and Decoding Ranking Test	Measurement	Subject-based Question Revision
Wednesday	• Animals	• Housing and Clothing • Housing and Clothing	• Air, Water and Rocks • Air, Water and Rocks	Achievers Section
Thursday	Revision: Science	Revision: Science	Revision: Science	Revision: Logical Reasoning
Friday	• Classification • Odd One Out	• Patterns • Problems Based on Figures	• Geometrical Shapes	Model Test Paper–1
Saturday	• Human Body	• Family and Festivals, Occupations	• Earth and Universe	Model Test Paper–2
Sunday	Self-Assessment Test (Duration: 3:00 hrs.)	Self-Assessment Test (Duration: 3:00 hrs.)	Self-Assessment Test (Duration: 3:00 hrs.)	Previous Years' NSO Papers.

NCO CLASS–2

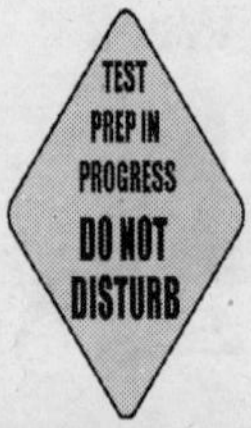	Week 1 	Week 2 	Week 3 	Week 4 
Day/Time	**Two Hours**	**Two Hours**	**Two Hours**	**Two Hours**
Monday	Introduction to Computer	• Uses of Computer	• Introduction to MS Paint	Revision (Subjective Section)
Tuesday	• Patterns • Series Completion	• Coding and Decoding Ranking Test	Grouping of Figures	Revision (Subjective Section)
Wednesday	• Fundamentals of Computer	Learning to Use Keyboard	• Latest Developments in IT	Revision (Achievers Section)
Thursday	Revision (Science)	Revision (Science)	Revision (Science)	Revision (Logical Reasoning)
Friday	• Odd One Out • Analogy	• Embedded Figures	• Measuring Units • Geometrical Shapes	Model Test Paper–1
Saturday	• Parts of a Computer	• Learning to Use Mouse	Revision	Model Test Paper–2
Sunday	Self-Assessment Test (Duration: 2:00 hrs.)	Self-Assessment Test (Duration: 2:00 hrs.)	Self-Assessment Test (Duration: 2:00 hrs.)	Previous Years' NCO Papers

IEO CLASS–2

	**WEEK 1** 	**WEEK 2** 	**WEEK 3** 	**WEEK 4** 
Day/Time	**Two Hours**	**Two Hours**	**Two Hours**	**Three Hours**
Monday	Spellings	Nouns	Articles	Tenses
Tuesday	Collocations	Pronouns	Articles	Reading Comprehension
Wednesday	Animals and Their Sounds	Verbs	Prepositions	Reading Comprehension
Thursday	Parts of Body and Clothes	Verbs	Conjunctions	Let's Speak
Friday	Basic Emotions	Adverbs	Punctuation	Model Test Paper–1
Saturday	Spellings	Adjective	Tenses	Model Test Paper–2
Sunday	Revision	Revision	Revision	Revision

Note:

- *Identify your weak areas through detailed reports and strengthen them.
- *Practice questions from huge question bank:
  - (i) MTG Workbooks for class 2
  - (ii) 'SOF Olympiad Trainer' Mobile Apps
  - (iii) OSDS (Olympiad Skill Development System)
- *Take more mock tests to improve your efficiency and become fully prepared for the exam.

7 Tips to Crack Olympiads

Tips to Crack Maths Olympiad

1. Focus on learning the concepts well and on acquiring the basic skills needed to solve problems.
2. Practise mathematics regularly. Make sure that you are solving as many different types of problems as possible. You can practise lots of questions on different topics from the Internet.
3. Identify the areas of your strength and weakness and focus on weak areas to get better results.
4. Solve model papers and understand the pattern of previous years' papers. This will help you to get acquainted with the pattern and structure of the test.
5. Learn shortcuts to solve various types of questions. Keep these points on your fingertips to save time and work efficiently.
6. Read questions thoroughly. Olympiad problems are known for their complexity, which means you have to take an extra effort.
7. During exam do not waste time in solving difficult questions; rather try some short and easy questions first.
8. Do a lot of practice covering each topic. After that take mock tests, analyse your result, and make an assessment report for your current score.
9. Prepare your notes and important facts to remember and do quick revision before exams. It helps in learning faster.

Tips to Crack Science Olympiad

1. Go through the concepts and ponder about them in a practical way.
2. Learn all the formulae and equations well and prepare notes for quick revision.
3. Do experiments in labs to practice and to learn the concepts well.

4. Learn and remember important shortcuts. They should be on your fingertips. It helps you save time and write answers efficiently.
5. Solve Previous Years Papers and Model Test Papers to understand the pattern and structure of the test.
6. Identify your weak areas and try to focus on the topics to overcome the difficulties.
7. Read every question well before answering. Some problems are typical in nature.
8. Do not waste your time in solving difficult questions. First take up easy questions and solve them.
9. Do quick revision before exams. It also helps in learning faster.

Tips to Crack Cyber Olympiad

1. Focus on learning the concepts well and on acquiring the basic skills needed to solve problems.
2. Make sure that you are doing as many different types of problems as possible.
3. Identify the areas of your strength and weakness and focus on weak areas to get better results.
4. Solve model papers and understand the pattern of previous years' papers. This will help you to get acquainted with the pattern and structure of the test.
5. Learn shortcuts to solve various types of questions. Keep these points on your fingertips to save time and work efficiently.
6. Read questions thoroughly. Olympiad problems are known for their complexity, which means you have to take an extra effort.
7. Do not waste time in solving difficult questions; rather try some short and easy questions first.
8. Do a lot of practice covering each topic. After that take mock tests, analyse your results, and make an assessment report for your current score.
9. Practise a lot of questions on different topics in the Olympiad syllabus from the Internet.
10. Prepare your notes and important facts to remember and do quick revision before exams. It helps in learning faster as well.

Tips to Crack English Olympiad

1. Read a newspaper every day. It will help you in understanding different types of sentence structures and will enhance your knowledge as well.
2. Go through one page of dictionary daily to enrich your vocabulary. This will add a lot of new words and their meanings in different contexts to your vocabulary.
3. Speak in English with your friends, parents and teachers. It will help you in learning verbal speaking skills.
4. Read grammar books and novels to learn language skills and grasp diverse contexts and themes.
5. Do a lot of practice on verbal and written English exercises daily.
6. Identify the areas of your strength and weakness and focus on weak areas to get better results.
7. Solve model papers and understand the pattern of previous years' papers. This will help you to get acquainted with the pattern and structure of the test.
8. Learn shortcuts to solve various types of questions. Keep these points on your fingertips to save time and work efficiently.
9. Read questions thoroughly. Olympiad problems are known for their complexity, which means you have to take an extra effort.
10. Do not waste time in solving difficult questions; rather try some short and easy questions first.
11. Prepare your notes and important facts to remember and to do quick revision before exams.

General Tips to Crack Olympiad

1. Go through the syllabus before you start preparation for the exam. For SOF Olympiad, you can visit the www.sofworld.org
2. Start preparations at least two months before the due schedule of the exam; go through all the curriculum books and study material.
3. Go through different books; solve questions that are a little tougher than traditional CBSE type questions.
4. Manage time properly. Time management skills can help you go through the exam successfully.
5. Consult your teachers. Approach your teachers and discuss your issues with him/her. He/she would certainly guide you.

6. Don't stress yourself. Take deep breaths, or eat your favourite ice-cream or even go for a long walk with your friend. Do anything that helps you relax before your exams. It is very important to keep your mind calm before any exam.
7. Read a little more text matter than that of your textbooks in order to gain better insight.
8. Just review everything in brief one day before beginning of the Olympiad test.

8 Study Material for Olympiads

Study Material and Coaching for IMO

The following books are recommended for preparation of the Olympiad test:

1. Challenges from the Olympiads by C.R. Pranesachar, S.A. Shirali, B.J. Venkatachala, and C.S. Yogananda
2. Problem Primer for the Olympiad by C.R. Pranesachar, B.J. Venkatachala, and C.S. Yogananda
3. You can also purchase the Olympiad Sample Papers for specific exam from www.classmantra.com. You will get the Practice Test and Mock Test.
4. You can purchase a series of books published by V&S Publishers to get precise study material and practice tests on all Olympiads – Mathematics, Science, Cyber, and English.

If any special coaching or tuition is required to become Olympiad Champion?

Though the series of IMO books published by V&S Publishers containing precise concepts with solved examples, illustrations, and diagrams is sufficient for self preparation, the students who find it difficult to learn on their own should go for special coaching/tuition.

Study Material and Coaching for NSO

The Olympiad resource books published by V&S Publishers for students of classes 1-10 are very useful for learning the concepts and for doing thorough practice. Each book consists of a lot Multiple Choice Questions based on theory, logical and analytical reasoning.

Salient features of each book:

- *Learning milestones* which enlists the topics covered in the chapter.
- *'Did You Know?'* provides extra information related to the chapter.
- *Test Your Skills and Activities* help children to explore their knowledge base.

- *Concept-based questions* are subjective and enhance the writing and learning skills of a student.
- *HOTS* also known as High Order Thinking Skills questions enrich the out-of-the-box thinking of children.
- Each exercise is divided into two sections:
  - (i) MCQs based on the chapter and syllabus
  - (ii) MCQS given in the Achievers section deal with extreme logics of the given chapter

If any special coaching or tuition is required to become Olympiad Champion?

Though the series of Science Olympiad books published by V&S Publishers, containing precise concepts with solved examples, illustrations, and diagrams is sufficient for self preparation, the students who find it difficult to learn on their own should go for special coaching/tuition.

Study Material and Coaching for NCO

The following books are recommended for Cyber Olympiad:

1. NCO – Olympiad Skill Development System (OSDS) by MTG
2. NCO – Workbooks for practice by MTG
3. BMA's Cyber Olympiad Resource Books

If any special coaching or tuition is required to become Olympiad Champion?

Though the series of Cyber Olympiad books published by V&S Publishers consisting of precise concept with solved examples and explanatory notes for difficult questions is sufficient for self-preparation, yet the students who find it difficult to learn on their own should go for special coaching/tuitions for studying the same.

Study Material and Coaching for IEO

If any special coaching or tuition is required to become Olympiad Champion?

Though the series of English Olympiad books published by V&S Publishers containing precise concepts with solved examples and illustrations are sufficient for self preparation, the students who find it difficult to learn on their own should go for special coaching/tuition.

9 Awards and Scholarships

During the academic year 2014-15, over 31500 schools from more than 1400 cities registered and millions of students appeared for the four Olympiad exams. These Olympiads were conducted across 19 countries. For the academic year 2015-16, the SOF will spend over Rupees ten crores on awards, scholarships, gifts and felicitations etc.

All the aspirants participating in IMO (1st level) get a Math Quotient (MQ), their scores and percentile, ranks at city, state, international levels, as well as a certificate of participation. SOF also prepares a performance report known as School Mathematics Quotient for all the participating schools.

The following awards will be provided to the winners of Olympiads being held during the academic year 2015-16.

Awards for Students/IMO Winners

- **For IMO, NSO, and NCO:** International and State toppers (in 20 zones/ states) of classes 3rd to 12th, the awards are given to 2nd level winners.
- **For IEO and winners of IMO, NSO, and NCO class 1st and 2nd:** International and State topper awards will be provided to 1st level winners.
- Each winner will be entitled to one award for an exam. The winners will be entitled to the higher level award only, i.e the international top 3 rank holders will be entitled to awards based on their International ranks. Awards accruing to them for State ranks will be given to the next rank holder. Similarly, school award accruing to a State award winner will be given to the next rank holder.
- All students scoring 100% marks in the 2nd level exams of IMO, NSO, and NCO (1st level exam in IEO) will win special awards consisting of gifts worth Rs.1000/ and Merit Certificates.

Scholarships and Merit Certificates

AT INTERNATIONAL LEVEL		
RANK	SCHOLARSHIP	NO.
1st	Rs.50,000/- each + Gold Medal* + Merit Certificate	47
2nd	Rs.25,000/- each + Silver Medal* + Merit Certificate	47
3rd	Rs.10,000/- each + Bronze Medal* + Merit Certificate	47
AT STATE LEVEL		
RANK	SCHOLARSHIP	NO.
1st	Rs5,000/ - each + Gold Medal* + Merit Certificate	940
2nd	Rs2500/ - each + Silver Medal* + Merit Certificate	940
3rd	Rs1000/ - each + Bronze Medal* + Merit Certificate	940
Rank 4th to 25th	Gifts Worth Rs.1000/- + Merit Certificate	20680

Medals at School Level: 600000 Medals to School Toppers:

- When 10 or more students from one class appear in the exam, *gold, silver and bronze medals are given to top 3 rank holders.
- When 5 to 9 students from a class appear in the exam,* gold medal is given to the top rank holder.

Student Performance Report (SPR)

- Every student who appears in any SOF Olympiad exam is provided with a Student Performance Report (SPR) which is a detailed analysis of how the student attempted in the 1st level Olympiad exam.
- The objective of SPR is to share analysis of performance in the exam with the student and her/his parents. This helps the student knows about the areas of his/her strengths and the areas for improvement on absolute terms and on competitive level consisting of peers from his/her class, who appeared for the Olympiad.

The SPR consists of seven sections:

- **Section A:** This section shows the marks obtained by a student and the rank achieved in school/city/state and at international level.
- **Section B:** This section reveals analysis of a student's performance in the Olympiad exams during past 6 years.
- **Section C:** This section consists of a topic-wise performance score of a student.

- **Section D**: This section provides correct answers to the questions asked in the Olympiad exam, the answers given by the student and performance analysis of student's answers with other students at state and international levels.
- **Section E:** This section provides a percentile score analysis of a student in comparison to class, state and international percentiles.
- **Section F:** This section shows analysis of average marks at school, state and international level.
- **Section G**: This section shows topic-wise performance comparison within a state.

Note:

(i) Participation certificate is given to every student.

(ii) Merit certification is given to 2nd level participants.

(iii) Medals are Gold/Silver/Bronze colour plated as applicable.

(iv) Top 25 rank holders from a class and each Olympiad exam will be awarded Gold Medals of Excellence and Merit Certificates of Excellence. This will be applicable for winners from 20 Zones/States for performance in the 1st level Olympiad in NCO, NSO, IMO and IEO.

Special Scholarships

- **Girl Child Scholarship Scheme (GCSS):** Rs.5000/- scholarship to 300 girls each, who are academically brilliant and come from economically weak families.
- **Scholarship for Excellence in English (SEE):** Rs.5000/- scholarship to 120 students each exhibiting excellence in English Language.
- **SOF Academic Excellence Scholarship (AES):** Rs.5000/ scholarship + Trophy to 160 students from class 3rd to class 10th. The student scoring highest number of marks in 3 Olympiad exams during one year/session wins the AES scholarship. The winners are selected from all 20 zones/ states.

Awards for Schools

	At International Level	
Category	**Awards**	**No. of Awards**
Best Principal	Rs.25000/- each + Citation + Trophy	10
Best Teacher	Rs.10000/- each + Citation + Trophy	40

At State Level		
Category	**Awards**	**No. of Awards**
Best Principal	Best Principal Rs.10000/- each + Citation + Trophy	100
Best Teacher	Best Teacher Rs.5000/- each + Citation + Trophy	240
At District Level		
Category	**Awards**	**No. of Awards**
Best Principal	Best Principal Rs.2500/- each + Citation + Trophy	300
Best Teacher	Best Teacher Rs.1000/- each + Citation + Trophy	650

School Performance Report (SPR)

- Every school which appears in any SOF Olympiad exam is provided with a School Performance Report (SPR) which is a detailed analysis of how the students in the school individually and in totality performed in the Olympiad exam.
- The objective of the report is to share analysis of performance of the students with the school authority. This helps the schools assess their strength and focus on the topics in which the students are weak in absolute terms and also on a competitive level vis-à-vis other schools.

The SPR consists of four parts:

1. **Part A:** This shows class-wise/student-wise marks and ranks achieved by students at the city, state and international level.
2. **Part B:** This provides topic-wise average school performance and comparison with other schools with standard deviation at school and international level.
3. **Part C:** This includes an average performance comparison of marks scored by students of a school versus marks scored by other students at the state and at international level.
4. **Part D:** This reveals the depth, section-wise comparison of performance of students of a school and students at state and international levels as well.

Note: Appreciation Mementos to School Principals and Teacher-in-Charge is given also.

10 Model Test Paper (IMO)

Section I : Logical Reasoning

1. Find the missing shape.

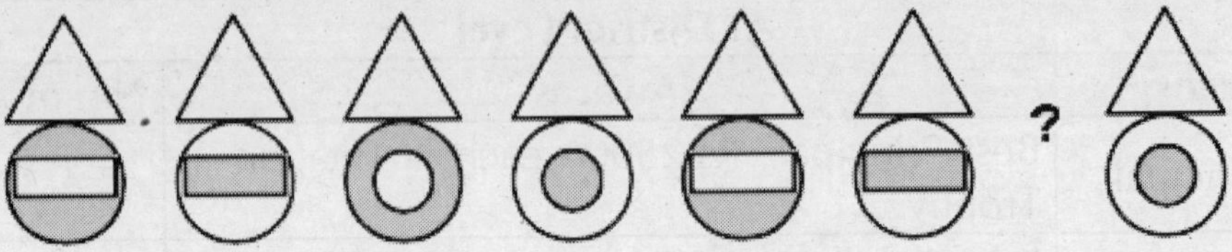

A. 

B. 

C. 

D. 

2. If Meeku jumps like this then what will be the next number on his stone?

A. 29 B. 28
C. 31 D. 27

3. How long did Golu take to complete his homework?

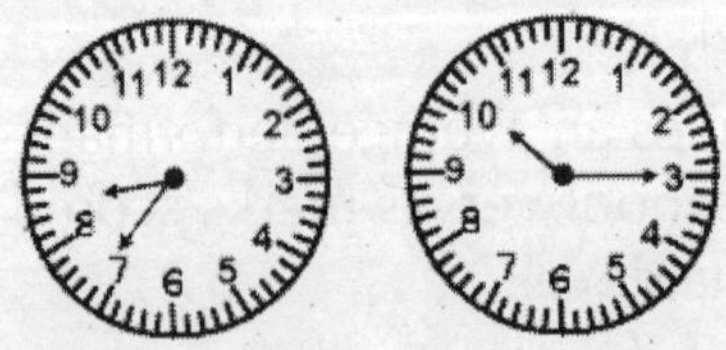

Started doing homework | Completed homework

A. 2 hours 20 minutes B. 2 hours
C. 1 hour 40 minutes D. 1 hour 20 minutes

4. Look at the two balance scales given below :

The mass of each  is _____ g.

A. 3 B. 10
C. 5 D. 15

5. Look at the Ashu's picture and tell how many different circles are there?

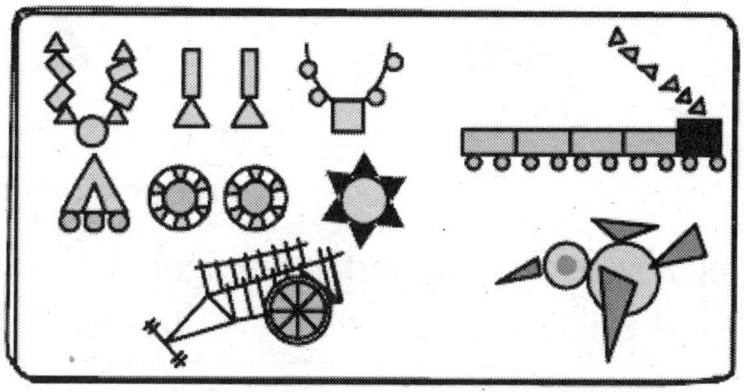

A. 24 B. 26 C. 28 D. 30

6. What is the length (in cm) of the pen?

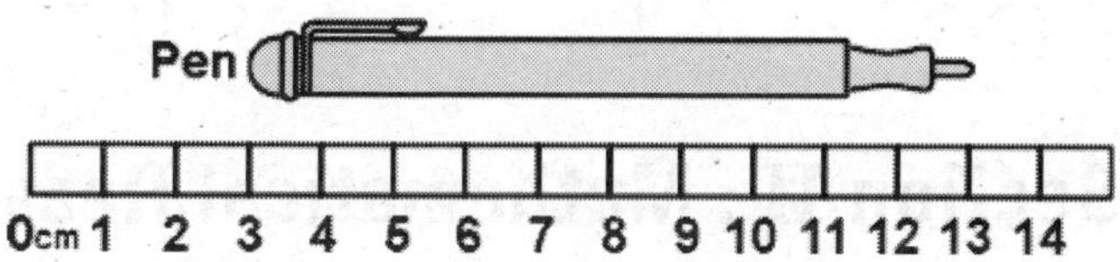

A. 13 cm B. 12 cm C. 10 cm D. 9 cm

7. Find the missing number.

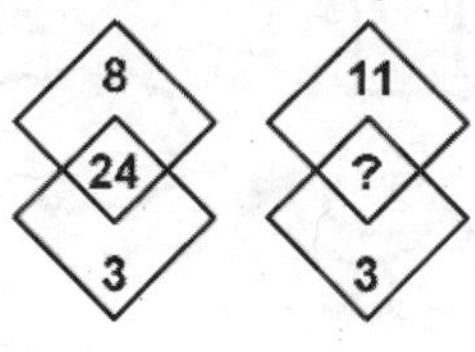

A. 12 B. 3 C. 28 D. 33

8. The hot dog is ________ g heavier than the humburger.

A. 100 B. 120 C. 140 D. 80

9. Which box is the lightest?

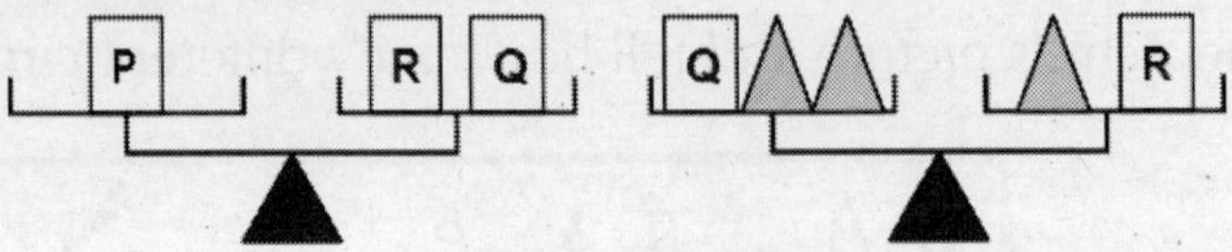

A. P B. Q

C. R D. Can't be determined.

10. How many rectangles can you find in the figure.

A. 8 B. 9 C. 11 D. 10

Section II : Mathematical Reasoning

11. Shraddha made some shapes in her picture. How many sleeping lines are there?

A. 1 B. 10 C. 3 D. 4

12. Which is the next figure in the given pattern?

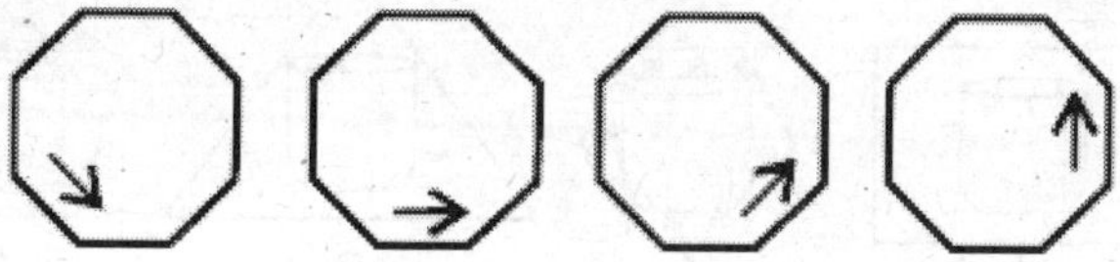

A. 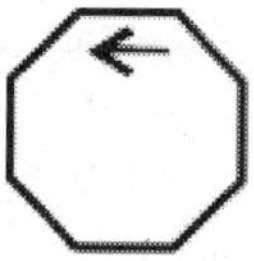

B. 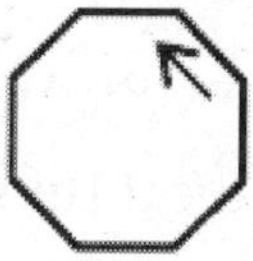

C. 

D. 

13. What is the number represented by each  ?

30 48 18

A. 6
B. 8
C. 10
D. 16

14. What is the missing number in the given pattern?

5A, 6B, 7C, ... 9E

A. 8D
B. 8C
C. 10E
D. 9D

15. I have 2 circular faces. I have a curved face. Soft drinks cans often look like me. What am I?

A. 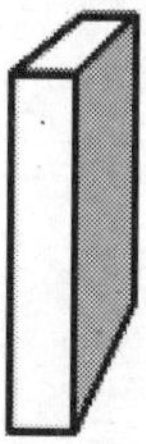

B. 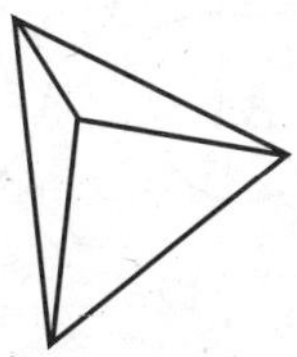

C. 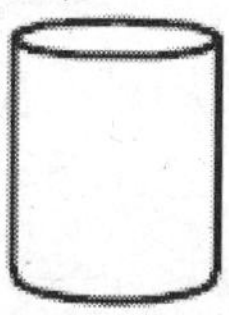

D. 

16. Which figure does not belong with the other three?

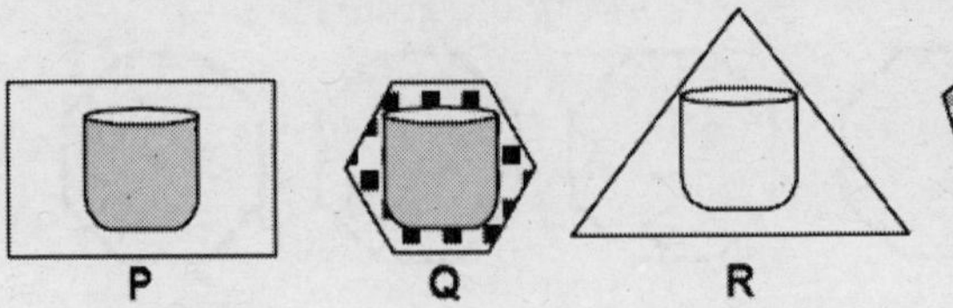

A. P B. Q C. R D. S

17. What will be the 11th shape in the pattern given below?

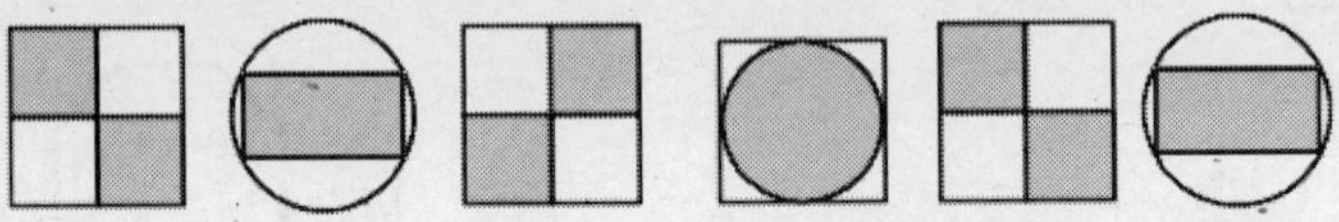

A. 

B. 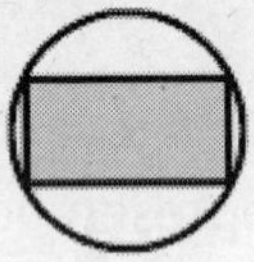

C. 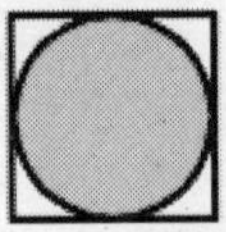

D. 

18. A papaya tree is 2 m shorter than the tree shown here. The total height of the papaya tree and the tree shown is __________ m.

A. 2 m B. 3 m C. 5 m D. 8 m

19. What is the difference of greatest and smallest number?

A. 24 B. 3 C. 32 D. 14

20. What fraction of the figure is shaded?

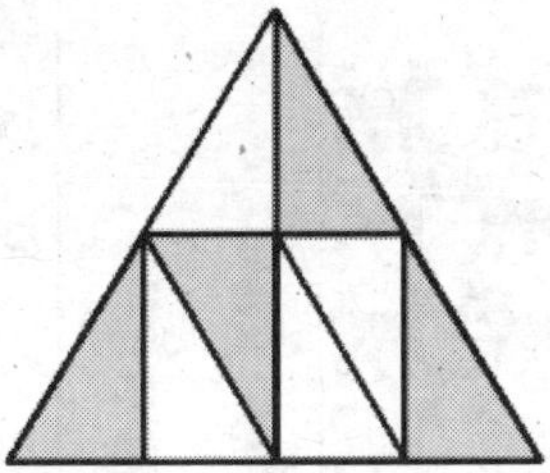

A. 2/3 B. 3/8

C. 4/12 D. 4/8

21. Mr. Mehra had 25 stamps. He shared the stamps equally among 5 boys. Each boy received _______________ stamps.

A. 5 B. 10

C. 32 D. 4823

22. Which of the following containers contain most amount of water?

A. Container A B. Container B

C. Container C D. Container D

23. Shraddha opened 4 new bottles of grape juice and poured the juice into glasses as shown below:

Bottle II contains 2 more glasses of grape juice than ___________

A. Bottle I B. Bottle II

C. Bottle IV D. None of these

24. The adjoining picture graph shows the number of each type of pet in Golu's pet shop. How many more fishes than cats does Golu's shop have?

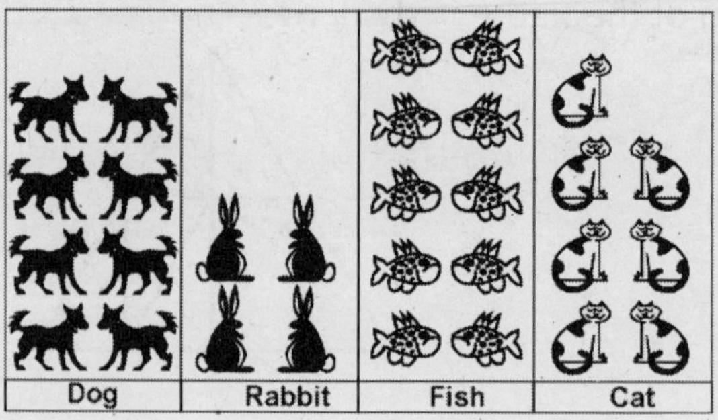

A. 7 B. 10

C. 3 D. 8

25. How many groups of 10 can these toy cars form?

A. 12 B. 2

C. 8 D. 6

Section III : Everyday Mathematics

26. How many months has 31 days?

A. 4 B. 8

C. 7 D. 6

27. Lisa saw 3 spiders in a garden. How many legs did she see in all?

A. 12 B. 24 C. 48 D. 36

28. I am a number between 25 + 5 and 21 + 3. What number am I?

A. 5 B. 7 C. 6 D. 9

29. 10 × ________ = 5 + 5 + 5 + 5 + 5 + 5 + 5 + 5 + 5 + 5

A. 10 B. 5 C. 0 D. 2

30. Golu made the adjoining picture graph. What is the total number of boys who play badminton and football?

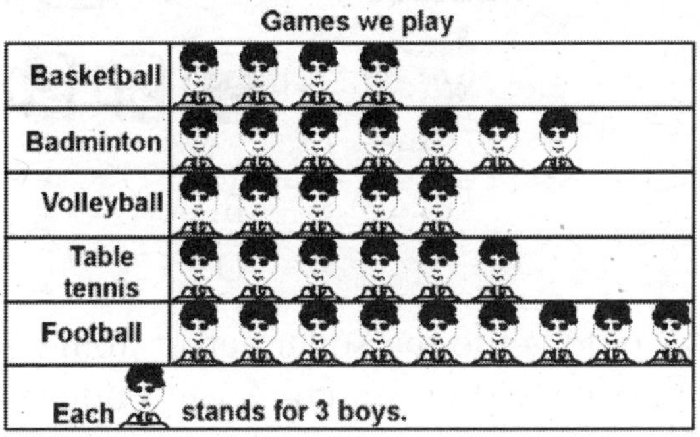

A. 12 B. 24 C. 16 D. 48

Section IV : Achievers Section

31. How many of these letters have both curves and straight lines?

A B C D E F G

A. 3 B. 2 C. 4 D. 6

32. I am a 2-digit number. My one's digit is 4 times my ten's digit. My ten's digit is 2. What am I?

A. 24 B. 28 C. 22 D. 42

33. The cost of each item is given below: If Jiah spent ₹ 348, what were the two items she bought?

A. The handbag and pair of shoes
B. The handbag and the dress
C. The dress and the pair of shoes
D. The pair of shoes and the necklace

34. A kettle of water can fill upto 3 teaspots. A teapot of water can fill up 4 cups. A kettle can fill up __________ cups.

A. 3
B. 8
C. 4
D. 12

35. Dia walks 512 m to get to the supermarket from her house. She has to walk another 128 m to get to the church. Aryan's house is 120 m farther from the church than Dia's house. How far is Aryan's house from the church?

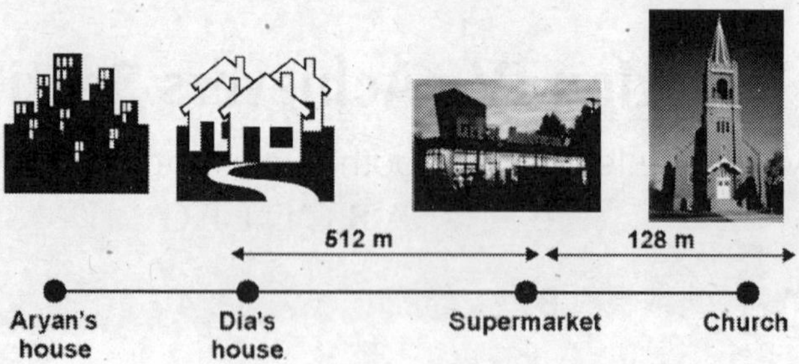

A. 192 m
B. 760 m
C. 640 m
D. 248 m

11 Model Test Paper (NSO)

1. Which of the following animal does not lay eggs?

A. 

B. 

C. 

D. 

2. Bees and butterflies collect ________ from flowers.

A. Colour
B. Oil
C. Nectar
D. All of these

3. Look at the given flow chart. Study it carefully.

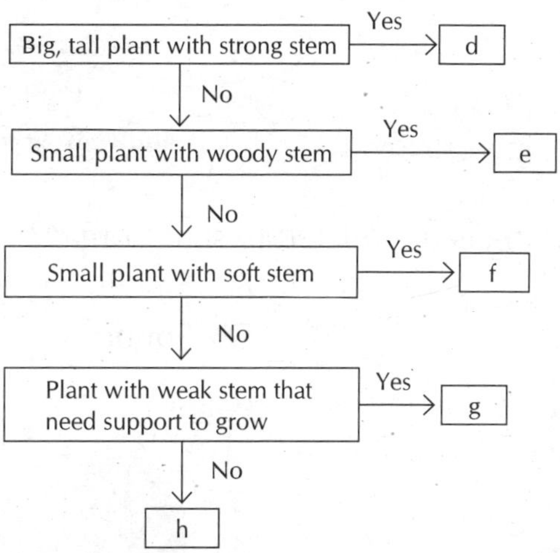

Which of the following statements is correct?

A. h represents coconut tree
B. g is a creeper
C. e is a shrub
D. d represents coriander plant

4. Which of the following are parts of a seed?

A. 

B. 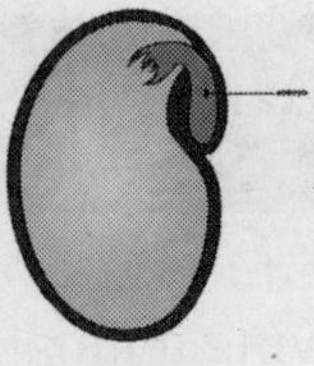

C. 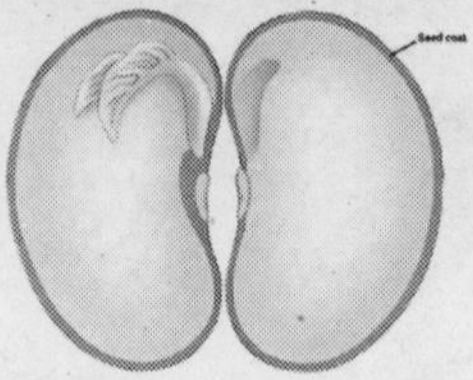

D. B and C both

5. Which organ(s) help us breathe?

A. 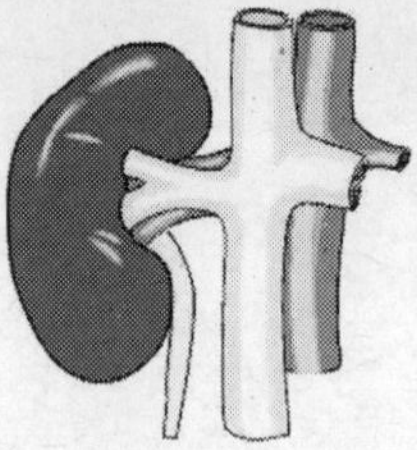

B. 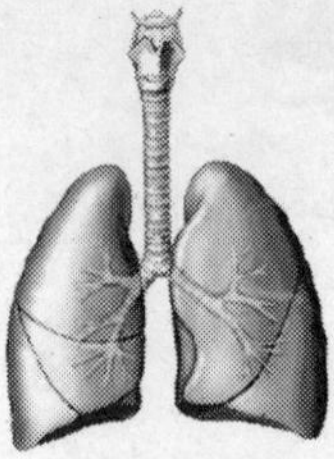

C. 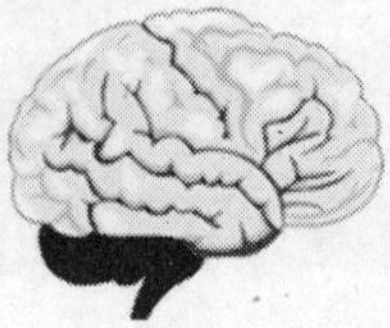

D. 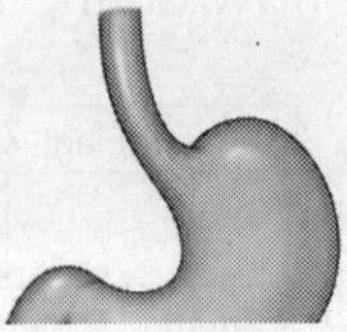

6. Which of the following is not related to sense organ?

A. Sight B. Smell

C. Digestion D. Sound

7. This fruit is used in making Indian beverages:

A. 

B. 

C. 

D. All of the above

8. Study the given flow chart and select the correct option which can fill the empty spaces "d", "e", and "f".

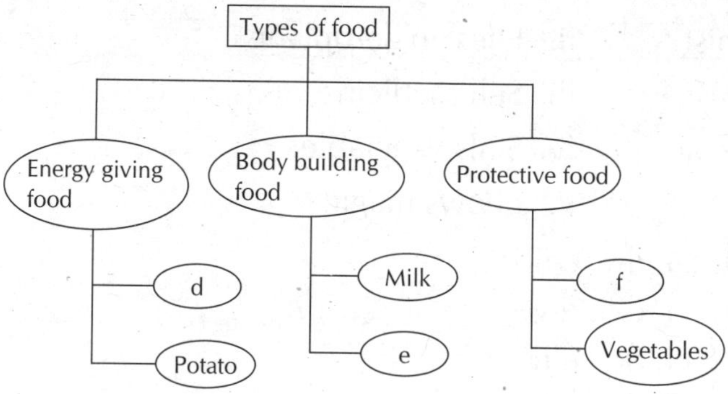

A. d-jaggery, e-butter, f-nuts
B. d-egg, e-fish, f-soyabean
C. d-rice, e-egg, f-nut
D. d-bread, e-fruits, f-cheese

9. In which of these places do people make light houses of wood and paper?

A. London
B. Mumbai
C. Kashmir
D. Japan

10. Which of the following can be run by gas engines?

1. 
2. 
3. 
4. 

A. 1 and 2
B. 1 and 4
C. 3 and 4
D. All of the above

11. Dussehra is celebrated on the ________ day of Navaratra.

A. 5th
B. 10th
C. 14th
D. 2nd

12. ________'s birthday is celebrated on 5th September.

A. Dr. Radhakrishnan
B. Dr. Rajendra Prasad
C. Bal Gangadhar Tilak
D. Lala Lajpat Rai

13. Match the following

a. Green-grocer	i. Baked bread
b. Chemist	ii. Flies an aeroplane
c. Baker	iii. Sell medicine
d. Magician	iv. Sells vegetables
e. Pilot	v. Shows magic

A. a-iv, b-iii, c-i, d-v, e-ii
B. a-iv, b-iii, c-i, d-ii, e-v
C. a-iv, b-i, c-iii, d-v, e-ii
D. a-iii, b-iv, c-i, d-v, e-ii

14. Ananya's school name is Ananya Juyal but at home everyone calls her Gauri. This other name is called:

A. Surname
B. First name
C. Nick name
D. Pet name

15. This person shown in the following picture is:

A. A person driving the car
B. A person making furniture
C. A person painting the car
D. A person painting the house

16. A person sells the items shown in the following image. Name the person.

A. Florist
B. Stationer
C. Grocer
D. Chemist

17. Which of these are incorrect statements regarding safety rules?
    1. Avoid swimming with grown-up near you
    2. Do not play rough games in the pool
    3. Always take a rubber tube with you
    4. Always swim in the deep end

A. 1 and 2
B. 1 and 4
C. 1, 2, and 4
D. All of them

18. Which of these is not a good habit?

A. Do not throw garbage on road
B. Throw waste into the dustbin
C. Always take excess food than needed
D. Keep food covered.

19. A ________ is a group of stars that forms an image.

A. Solar system
B. Constellation
C. Planet
D. The Sun

20. At which the Moon be during an eclipse of the Sun?

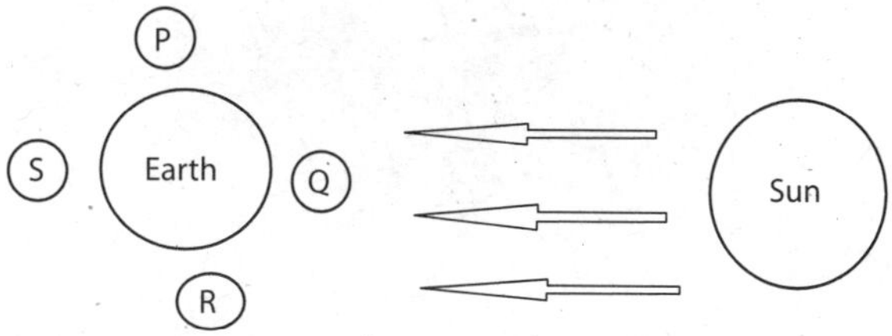

A. R
B. Q
C. P
D. S

21. Which common thing, the following objects need?

A. Thread
B. Sun
C. Water
D. Air

22. Which statement is true?

A. Air has no weight
B. Air stays in one place
C. Air takes up space
D. Air is blue in colour

23. Identify the following instrument:

A. Wind vane
B. Lactometer
C. Balance
D. Rain gauge

24. In how many states can water exist?

A. 1 B. 2

C. 3 D. 4

25. Which fibre is used to make a sweater?

A. 

B. 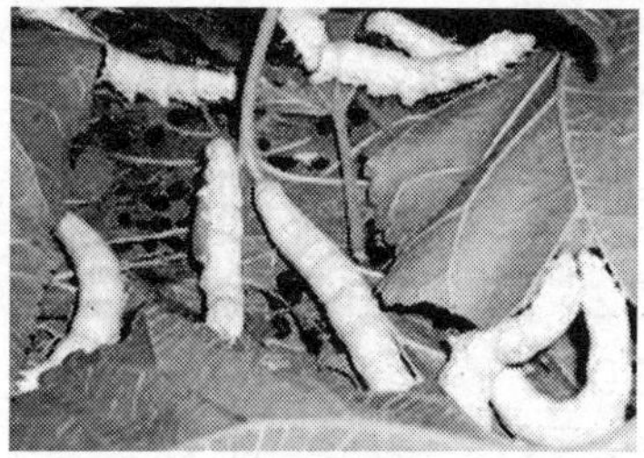

C. 

D. 

Answer Key

1. B; 2. C; 3. C; 4. D; 5. B; 6. C; 7. D; 8. C; 9. D; 10. A;
11. B; 12. A; 13. A; 14. C; 15. B; 16. C; 17. B; 18. C; 19. B; 20. B;
21. D; 22. C; 23. A; 24. C; 25. C

12 Model Test Paper (NCO)

Reasoning

1. What is the missing number?

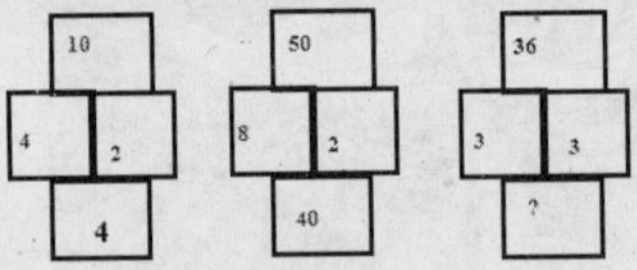

(A) 32 (B) 42
(C) 30 (D) 33

2. Find the odd one out.

(A) ABCE (B) #dgfr567#@!!

(C abugd (D) !@#^$%$

3. How many slanting lines are there in the given figure?

(A) 14 (B) 20
(C) 18 (D) 12

4. Match column-I with column-II to get the sum of the numbers as 50.

Colum-I	Column-II
(i) 22	(a) 25
(ii) 15	(b) 28
(iii) 25	(c) 35
(iv) 45	(d) 5

(A) i-b, ii-c, iii-a, iv-d
(B) i- a, ii-c, iii-b, iv-d
(C) i-b, ii-d, iii-a, iv-c
(D) i-c, ii-b, iii-d, iv-a

5. Use the skip-counting method to find the missing numbers.

Value of 1 candy = 15

(A) 45, 60, 90 (B) 15, 40, 55
(C) 40, 55, 60 (D) 30, 45, 60

6. Look at the number cloud. The lowest 4 digit number that can be formed without repeating the digits is ______.

(A) 2015 (B) 1025
(C) 1250 (D) 2150

7. The given figure is made up of _____ straight lines and ______ curved lines, respectively.

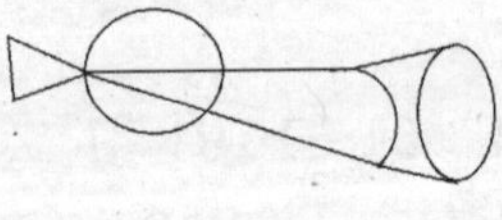

(A) 7, 6 (B) 6, 7
(C) 7, 8 (D) 5, 6

8. The given picture shows ________.

(A) 3 groups of 3 dolls
(B) 4 groups of 4 dolls
(C) 4 groups of 3 dolls
(D) 3 groups of 4 dolls

9. Rohit and Sonia are going to visit their grandparents in their village and then they will go to a hill station for holidays. They have made (✓) and (✧) marks on the calendar for the days they will spend with their grandparents and in the hill station, respectively.

How many days will they spend in the hill station (I) and with their grandparents (II), respectively?

June						
Mon	Tue	Wed	Thu	Fri	Sat	Sun
	1	2	3	4	5	6
7	8	9	10	11	12	13
14	15 ✓	16 ✓	17 ✓	18 ✓	19 ✓	20 ✓
21 ✧	22 ✧	23 ✧	24 ✧	25	26	27
28	29	30				

	I	II		I	II
(A)	4	6	(B)	6	4
(C)	7	7	(D)	4	4

10. Look at the figures given below.

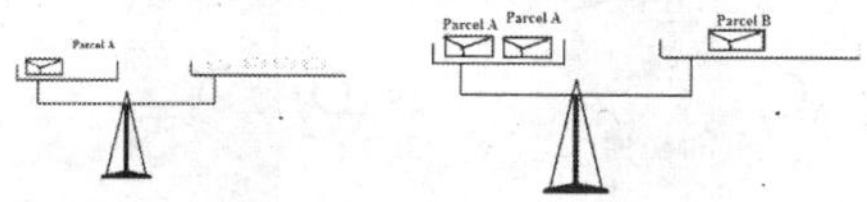

If 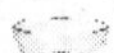 weighs 100 gm, what is the weight of parcel B?

(A) 900 gm (B) 800 gm
(C) 500 gm (D) 700 gm

11. There are 70 roses in rows of 10 in a garden. How many roses are there in each column?

(A) 17 (B) 70
(C) 77 (D) 7

12. Sanchit wants to finish his homework within 30 min. He began at 3:15 p.m, but he took 10 minutes more than 30 minutes. At what time did he stop?

(A) 3:45 p.m. (B) 3:35 p.m.
(C) 3:55 p.m. (D) 4:15 p.m.

13. Read the given table and find the value of P, Q, R and S respectively.

Total money in hand	Purchase	Remaining Amount
 (P)	 Rs. 280	P – Q = R
	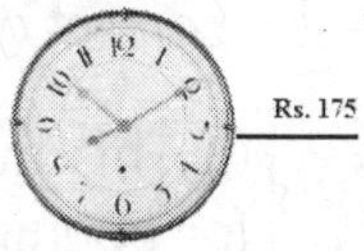 Rs. 175	P – 175 = S

(A) 300, 270, 20, 125
(B) 300, 220, 20, 125
(C) 300, 125, 20, 280
(D) 300, 280, 20, 125

14. There are 200 cows in a farm. How many legs are there in all?

(A) 400 (B) 800
(C) 1600 (D) 1200

15. If tomorrow is Monday, then yesterday was ______.

(A) Saturday (B) Sunday
(C) Friday (D) Wednesday

Computers

1. Who am I?

   (a) I am a part of computer.

   (b) I am used to store the files.

   I am also known as ___________.

   (A) Files/drives

   (B) Folders/dictionary

   (C) Directory, folders

   (D) Files/folders

2. Reena works in a multinational company. She is required to visit many places for her office work. Which kind of computer is most useful and helpful for her?

   (A) Supercomputer

   (B) Mainframe computer

   (C) Desktop

   (D) Laptop

3. Match column I and column II and choose the correct option.

a. ALT+F4	(i) This button is used for opening programs, documents, control panel and turning off the computer
b. Maximise button	(ii) The taskbar does not display this button
 c.	(iii) We can close a program by pressing this button
d. Windows	(iv) an operating system

   (A) a-i, b-iii, c-ii, d-iv

   (B) a-iii, b-ii, c-i, d-iv

   (C) a-i, b-ii, c-iii, d-iv

   (D) a-iv, b-ii, c-iii, d-i

4. This type of wire is used to connect a computer to a mobile phone.

   (A)  (B) 

   (C) 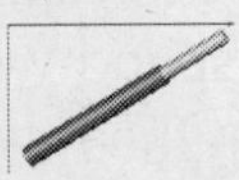 (D) 

5. Sanchit wants to watch a movie on his computer. He switched ON theCPU. The CPU gets started but the desktop was not display anything. Which of the followings could be the reason(s)?

   i. No electricity

   ii. UPS not working

   iii. Display button of monitor switched OFF

   iv. No power supply in the monitor

   (A) i and iv (B) iv only

   (C) iii and iv only (D) iii only

6. Rahul has lost a file. Which option can help him find his lost file?

   (A) 

   (B) 

   (C) 

   (D) 

7. Identify the object.

   (a) Originated in China, 3000 years ago

   (b) Used as calculating machine

   (A) Robot

   (B) Abacus

   (C) Pascal

   (D) CPU

8. Matchcolumn I and column II and choose the correct option.

Column-I	**Column-II**
(i) F1 key	(a) used to renames files and folders
(ii) F2 key	(b) used as the help key
(iii) F5 key	(c) used for navigation in Microsoft Office
(iv) F6 key	(d) used to "Find and Replace" words in

(A) i-b, ii-a, iii-d, iv-c
(B) i-c, ii-a, iii-d, iv-b
(C) i-b, ii-c, iii-d, iv-a
(D) i-b, ii-d, iii-a, iv-c

9. Look at the picture below. It is a set of keys of a keyboard. This set is called ______.

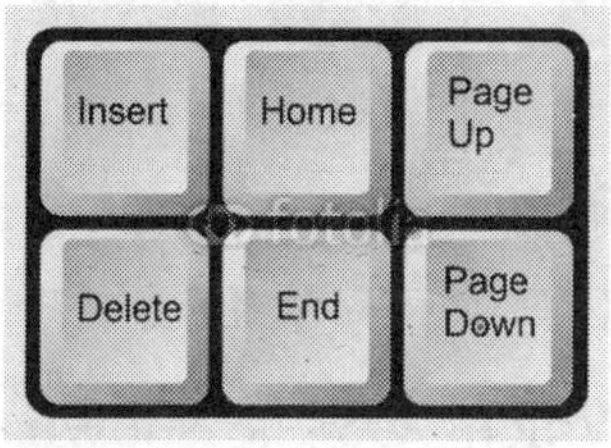

(A) Navigation keys
(B) Function keys
(C) Arrow keys
(D) Special keys

10. Optical mouse used this type of technique.
(A) The laser technique
(B) Mouse-pad technique
(C) Optomechanical technique
(D) Mechanical technique

11. Click and drag process is:
(A) Clicking the left and right mouse buttons and dragging the mouse without releasing it
(B) Clicking the right mouse button and dragging the mouse without releasing it
(C) Clicking the left mouse button and dragging the mouse without releasing it
(D) Clicking the drag button of the mouse and dragging the mouse without releasing it

12. Ritu is drawing a picture in MS Paint. She wants to erase a part of it but due to the small size of her eraser tool, she is taking a lot of time. She wants to enhance the size of eraser tool. Which of the following key combination will help her?
(A) Alt + Numpad
(B) Shift + Numpad
(C) Ctrl + Numpad
(D) Tab + Numpad

13. Matc column I and column II and choose the correct option.

Column-I	**Column-II**
(a) 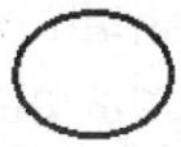	(i) pentagon tool
(b) 	(ii) Rounded rectangle tool
(c) 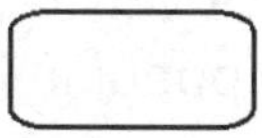	(iii) Rounded rectangle call out tool
(d) 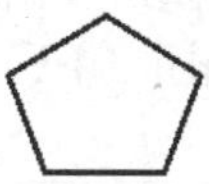	(iv) Oval tool

(A) a-i, b-iii, c-ii, d-iv
(B) a-iii, b-iv, c-ii, d-i
(C) a-iv, b-ii, c-iii, d-i
(D) a-iv, b-iii, c-ii, d-i

14. Who am I?

(a) I belong from the Google group.

(b) I am a free video chat service.

(A) Wi-Fi

(B) Google hangout

(C) A social networking site

(D) An android application

15. This is not a mouse type.

(A) Fibre mouse

(B) Optical Mouse

(C) Three-button mouse

(D) Wireless Mouse

Achievers Section

16. Match column I and column II and select the correct option:

(I) What is iPad Mini?

(II) What is iPod Nano?

	Column-I	Column-II
A.	Smaller lighter version of the Apple iPad tablet	A small portable media player produced by Apple Inc.
B.	Smaller lighter version of the Apple iPod	A version of the popular iTunes
C.	Smaller lighter version of the Apple iPhone	Apples latest tablet PC
D.	All of these	Apples latest mobile phone

17. Seema has made a picture on MS Paint. Now she wants to take a printout. Under which section she will find the Print Option?

(A) 

(B) 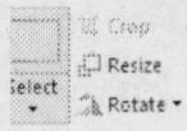

(C) 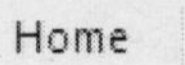

(D) 

18. Which of the following matches is incorrect?

(A) Diagnosis diseases — (i) Computer in hospital

(B) Watching movies — (ii) Computer for entertainment

(C) For communication — (iii) Computers in defense

(D) Watching sports — (iv) Computers in school

19. Look at the icons below. How many are multimedia icons?

(A) 1 (B) 3

(C) 2 (D) 0

20. (I) Which OS is shown on the desktop below?

(II) How many word files are open in the computer, how will you know?

	I	II
(A)	Win 8	We will left click on the MS Word icon.
(B)	Win 7	We will left click on the MS Word icon.

(C) Win 8	We will just place the mouse cursor on the MS word icon in the taskbar.	(D) Win 7	We will just place the mouse cursor on the MS word icon in the taskbar.

Answer Key

1.(C)	2.(B)	3.(A)	4.(A)	5.(D)	6.(B)	7.(A)	8.(C)
9.(A)	10.(B)	11.(D)	12.(C)	13.(D)	14.(B)	15.(A)	
1.(B)	2.(D)	3.(B)	4..(A)	5.(C)	6.(B)	7.(B)	8.(A)
9.(A)	10.(A)	11.(C)	12.(C)	13.(D)	14.(B)	15.(A)	
1.(A)	2.(A)	3.(D)	4.(C)	5.(C)			

13 Model Test Paper (IEO)

Section I : Word And Structure Knowledge

Directions (1 – 4) : Choose the word with correct spelling.

1. A. Fourtune B. Fortune C. Phortune D. Forteune
2. A. Successful B. Sucesful C. Succesfull D. Successful
3. A. Deceve B. Desieve C. Decieve D. Deceive
4. A. Grammer B. Grammar C. Gramar D. Gramer

Directions (5 – 8) : Match the word with correct option and find out the correct alternative.

5. Hand
   A. Leg B. Face C. Arm D. Ear
6. Table
   A. Chair B. Flower C. Plate D. Tablecloth
7. Lock
   A. Car B. Window C. Door D. Key
8. Doctor
   A. House B. School C. Hospital D. Playground

Directions (9 – 12) : Find the odd word from the options given below.

9. A. Cow B. Goose C. Dog D. Bike
10. A. Fields B. Story C. Forests D. Woods
11. A. Daisy B. Laptop C. Phone D. Computer
12. A. Mother B. Brother C. Teacher D. Grandfather

Directions (13 – 20) : Select the right word to fill in the blank.

13. Shah Rukh Khan is a ________ Bollywood actor.
    A. Ugly B. Unknown C. New D. Famous
14. There are ________ in the forests.
    A. Tigers B. Pens C. Cars D. Stairs
15. Geeta won the Art competition. She is so ________.
    A. Funny B. Mean C. Creative D. Sad
16. A ________ is when people go for a holiday on a boat.
    A. Road trip B. Cruise C. Tour D. Drive
17. The volunteers ________ a bridge.
    A. Built B. Made C. Created D. Prepared
18. When Mr. Singh reached home, he ________his door
    A. Entered B. Locked C. Rung D. Unlocked
19. He ______the child from drowning
    A. Fainted B. Stopped C. Helped D. Saved
20. The police ________ the thief.
    A. Left B. Caught C. Catched D. Helped

SECTION II : Reading

Gandhi Jayanti is celebrated yearly on 2nd October. It is one of the three official declared national holidays of India and is observed in all of its states and union territories. The other two national holidays are Independence Day (15th August) and Republic Day (26th January).

Gandhi Jayanti is marked by prayer services and tributes all over India, especially at Raj Ghat, Gandhi's memorial in New Delhi where he was cremated. Popular activities include prayer meetings, commemorative ceremonies in different cities by colleges, local government institutions and socio-political institutions. Painting and essay competitions are conducted and best awards are granted for projects in schools and the community on themes of glorifying peace, non-violence and Gandhi's effort in Indian Freedom Struggle.

On the basis of the above paragraph, complete the sentences.

21. Gandhi Jayanti is celebrated on ___________.
    A. 12 October B. 2 October
    C. 2 June D. 4 November
22. How many national holidays are there?
    A. 4 B. 2
    C. 3 D. 1
23. Where is Raj Ghat located?
    A. New Delhi B. Lucknow
    C. Kolkata D. Chennai
24. How do schools celebrate?
    A. Writings songs
    B. Athletic meets
    C. Races
    D. Paintings and Essay competitions
25. Prayer meetings and commemorative ceremonies are held by
    A. Colleges, Government bodies and others
    B. Families
    C. Hospital
    D. Schools
26. To glorify means:
    A. To make beautiful
    B. Describe or represent as admirable
    C. To demean
    D. To praise

Dear Annie,

In today's fast world, it's difficult to find a true friend like you. I sometimes think I am very lucky to get you as one; without you life would have been very boring. I still remember the first day of school when we were young, you called me and gave a seat besides you. It's now almost 15 years and our relationship has grown in past years. I would like to thank you for being there for me through the ups and downs of my life.

Last year when my father fell ill, you were a support to me and my family. I don't know what I would have done without you then. You were more helpful than my relatives .I can never forget how you stayed back in the hospital late night just to support me and my mother.

I cherish every moment of life we spent together. Though you are away from me, I still feel that you are close to me. How are your studies going? Last time when you wrote you seemed little worried about the portions. I know you will easily pass your engineering course with flying colours.

When are your next holidays? I am eagerly waiting to meet you and spend some good time together.

I would like to thank you for being my friend and being there for me.

With best wishes,

Tarun.

On the basis of the above paragraph, answer the following questions.

27. Who is Annie to Tarun?
    A. Boss B. Best Friend
    C. Cousin D. Sister

28. How long have they known each other?
    A. 15 years B. 10 years
    C. 7 years D. 13 ears

29. What happened the last year to Tarun ?
    A. He got promoted
    B. He got Married
    C. He got a dog
    D. His father fell ill.

30. What is Annie worried about?
    A. Her sister
    B. Her job
    C. Her Engineering exams
    D. Her plants

31. What does Tarun hope to do when he meets Annie next?
    A. Thank her for being his friend
    B. Take her for a movie
    C. Have lunch together
    D. Go for a picnic

SECTION III : Spoken And Written Expression

Direction (32 – 35) : Choose the best reply to complete each conversation.

32. Peter: What a beautiful lake!
    Sam:
    A. Not really
    B. I don't care for lakes
    C. It's okay
    D. It really is!

33. Anita: May I speak to Lena?
    Monica:
    A. No
    B. Yes, please hold while I get her.
    C. She doesn't want to
    D. I can't call her

34. Bert: Hello, I'm Bert.
    Ernie:
    A. Hello, my name is Ernie.
    B. I don't care
    C. So?
    D. Hmmm, I'm Ernie

35. Rachel: How do you do?
    Tom:
    A. Not very well
    B. Okay.
    C. Good and how are you?
    D. I don't want to answer

Answer Key

1. B; 2. A; 3. D; 4. B; 5. C; 6. A; 7. D; 8. C; 9. D; 10. B;
11. A; 12. C; 13. D; 14. A; 15. C; 16. C; 17. A; 18. D; 19. D; 20. B;
21. B; 22. C; 23. A; 24. D; 25. A; 26. D; 27. B; 28. A; 29. D; 30. C;
31. A; 32. D; 33. B; 34. A; 35. C

English Olympiad

Jumbled Words ★ Words and Their Meanings ★ Words and Their Opposites ★ Identifying a Word from the Picture ★ Making a Word ★ Feminine and Masculine ★ One and Many ★ Word Pairs ★ Odd One Out ★ Animals and Their Young Ones ★ Nouns ★ Verbs ★ Articles ★ A Ball For My Dog ★ Buzz, Buzz Bumblebee ★ Rock Band ★ High Order Thinking Skills (HOTS) ★ Short Answer Questions ★ Model Test Paper - 1 ★ Model Test Paper - 2 ★ Model Test Paper - 3 ★ Model Test Paper - 4 ★ Model Test Paper - 5

Spellings ★ Collocations ★ Animals and Their Sounds ★ Parts of Body and Clothes ★ Basic Emotions ★ Nouns ★ Pronouns ★ Verbs ★ Adverbs ★ Adjective ★ Articles ★ Prepositions ★ Conjunctions ★ Punctuation ★ Simple Tenses ★ Tips on Reading Comprehension ★ Let's Speak ★ High Order Thinking Skills (HOTS) ★ Short Answer Questions ★ Model Test Paper - 1 ★ Model Test Paper - 2

Spellings ★ Collocations ★ Animals and Their Sounds ★ Household Things ★ Food and Clothes ★ Basic Emotions ★ Word Power ★ Nouns ★ Pronouns ★ Verbs ★ Adverbs ★ Proverbs ★ Adjectives ★ Noun: Number and Gender ★ Articles ★ Prepositions ★ Conjunctions ★ Tenses ★ Modal Verbs ★ Punctuations ★ Tips on Reading Comprehension ★ Tips for Good Conversation ★ High Order Thinking Skills (HOTS) ★ Short Answer Questions ★ Model Test Paper - 1 ★ Model Test Paper - 2

Spellings ★ Collocations ★ Animals and Pets ★ Household Things ★ Food and Clothes ★ Basic Emotions ★ Synonyms and Antonyms ★ Nouns ★ Pronouns ★ Verbs ★ Modals ★ Adverbs ★ Adjectives ★ Contractions ★ Articles ★ Prepositions ★ Conjunctions ★ Tenses ★ Jumbled Words ★ Tips on Reading Comprehension ★ Tips for Good Conversation ★ High Order Thinking Skills (HOTS) ★ Short Answer Questions ★ Model Test Paper - 1 ★ Model Test Paper - 2

Spelling ★ Collocation and Idioms ★ Homonyms and Homophones ★ Words Related to Feelings ★ Food and Travel ★ Health, Appearance and Character ★ Noun ★ Pronoun ★ Verbs ★ Adverbs ★ Adjectives ★ Articles ★ Prepositions ★ Punctuations ★ Tenses ★ Passive Voice ★ Reported Speech ★ Reading Comprehension ★ Let's Speak ★ High Order Thinking Skills (HOTS) ★ Model Test Paper - 1 ★ Model Test Paper - 2

visit our online bookstore: **www.vspublishers.com**